Phonics Tales!

sh

Shelly's New Shoes

by Pamela Chanko
illustrated by Doug Jones

SCHOLASTIC INC.

New York • Toronto • London • Auckland • Sydney
Mexico City • New Delhi • Hong Kong • Buenos Aires

Designed by Maria Lilja
ISBN-13: 978-0-439-88474-7 • ISBN-10: 0-439-88474-8
Copyright © 2006 by Scholastic Inc.
All rights reserved. Printed in the U.S.A.

First printing, September 2006

12 11 10 9 8 7 6 5 4 3 2 1   6 7 8 9 10 11/0

P9-DGT-283

Phonics Fact

Sh is a digraph. Digraphs are two letters put together to make a single sound, such as the *sh* sound in **Shelly**, **shirt**, and **shorts**. What other *sh* words can you find in this story? Look at the pictures, too!

This is **Shelly**. **She** has a favorite **shirt** and **shorts**.

Shelly also has some favorite **shoes**. **She** thinks
they are really **sharp**!

One day, **Shelly** got a **shock**. She **pushed** and **shoved** her feet into her **shoes**. But her **shoes** did not fit!

SH Cheer

Hooray for *s-h*, the best sound around!

Let's holler *s-h* words all over town!

There's **shoe** and **shelf** and **splash** and **wish**.

There's **shop** and **shirt** and **push** and **fish**.

There's **shell** and **shorts** and **crush** and **dash**.

There's **shape** and **ship** and **shout** and **smash**.

S-h, s-h, give a great cheer,

For the **shiniest** sound you ever will hear!

Make a list of other words that have *sh* at the beginning or the end. Then use them in your cheer.

SH Riddles

Listen to the riddles. Then match each with the right *sh* word from the box. (Hint: Sometimes the *sh* appears at the end of the word.)

Word Box

cash	shut	fish	shelf	shorts
wish	shoes	shirt	ship	shape

1. You wear these on your feet.

2. This animal has gills and swims.

3. You make one when you blow out your birthday candles.

4. It has sleeves and a collar.

5. You wear these when it's too hot for long pants.

6. This is another word for *money*.

7. You can put books on this.

8. This word means the opposite of *open*.

9. It sails across the sea.

10. It can be a triangle, a square, or a circle.

15

"I know. They are really **sharp**!" **gushed Shelly**.
"We'll take the red **shoes**," said Mom to the
shopkeeper. "Isn't that a **shock**?"

But then **Shelly** spotted one last pair on the top **shelf** in the **shadows**.
"**Gosh**," said Mom, "those look just like your old **shoes**!"

Shelly **shut** her eyes and **shed** a tear.
"I **wish** I didn't need new **shoes**!" **she** cried.

Shelly tried on every **shoe** in the **shop**. But the **shoes** were either too **showy**, or too **shaky**, or they gave her a **rash**.

Next, he **showed Shelly** some sandals covered in **seashells**.
"These **crush** my toes!" **she** said.

Then, he **showed Shelly** some pointy **shoes**.
"I don't like the **shape**!" **she** said.

First, he **showed Shelly** some fancy **shoes**.
"Too **shiny**!" **she** said.

"I have many **shoes** to **show** you," said the
shopkeeper. "We have **shelves** and **shelves**
of **shoes**!"

"We **should** go **shopping**," Mom said. So **she** grabbed **Shelly** and **dashed** to **Sherman's shoe shop**.

"These **shoes** are going in the **trash**!" Mom said.
"No!" **shouted** Shelly.